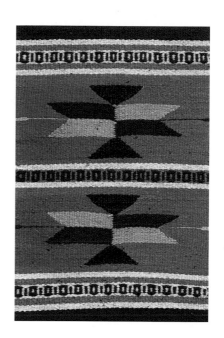

mexican

style source book

photography by Peter Aprahamian

text by Susan Tomlinson

Mexican Style

creative ideas for enhancing your space

UNIVERSE

I would especially like to thank the following people for all
their help and hospitality in Mexico: José Luis Cortes, Folke
S. Egerström, Pedro Friederburg, Agustin Hernandez, Enrique
Martin-Moreno, Elvia Navarro (Sectur), Eduardo Prieto,
Rodolfo Rogarrio, Norma Soto (Barragán Foundation), and
José de Yturbe. I would also like to thank the many people I
met during my travels who cannot be named but were always
friendly, enthusiastically helpful, and who showed me the true
spirit of their wonderful country. *Peter Aprahamian*

First published in the United States of America in 2000
by Universe Publishing
A Division of Rizzoli International Publications, Inc.
300 Park Avenue South
New York, NY 10010

© 2000 MQ Publications Ltd
Photographs © 2000 Peter Aprahamian

98 99 00 01 02 / 10 9 8 7 6 5 4 3 2 1

Printed in Italy

contents

Any study of Mexican style involves a journey through the past. Over the course of 3000 years Mexico has witnessed much bloodshed and upheaval. With every new battle and reigning civilization, another mark is drawn on the cultural map, and more artistic influences emerge.

2

introduction

The first known civilization, existing around 1500 B.C., was the Olmecs of Southern Veracruz. With stone as their canvas, and using nothing more than simple tools of volcanic glass and obsidian, they carved enormous stone heads, some almost 6 feet high.

By far the most influential civilization of southern Mexico was the Maya, existing around 600 B.C. Theirs was the first society to build stepped pyramids and huge stone palaces. The Zapotecs, a priest-dominated society, emerged around the same time, building the hilltop metropolis of Monte Albán outside Oaxaca. The largest metropolis of pre-Hispanic Mexico is Teotihuacán. Founded in A.D. 50, the ruins lie some 27 miles northeast of Mexico City. Archaeologists don't know for sure the ethnic identity of those who established it, but when it was found abandoned by the Aztecs, it became known as "The Birthplace of the Gods." The famous Pyramid of the Sun towers over the dusty Avenue of the Dead, the city's main street.

The Toltecs are the enigma of the pre-Hispanic cultures. It is thought they moved into the Valley of Anáhuc (now the site of Mexico City) after the fall of

1 The Spanish count who built this eighteenth-century mansion wanted his house to be in the popular style at a time when Mexico was looking towards France for stylistic guidance. The sweeping staircase and decorative balcony could feature easily in a French mansion, except for the telltale bright red walls and handmade saddles.

2 A papier mâché lady with a flower in her hair reflects the exuberant color and spirit of Mexico.

◁ 1

Teotihuacán, establishing their capital city, Tula. This city was so influential, it became a legend among subsequent civilizations, such as the Aztecs who followed them into the valley. This civilization considered itself to be the chosen one. Within 300 years they had established a huge empire, terrifying in its domination and religious beliefs, with the city of Tenochtitlán as their center.

Pre-Hispanic Mexico had existed in isolation for thousands of years but with the arrival of the Spanish, Mexico felt the impact of the rest of the world within a few short years. Arriving in 1519, it took just three years for Cortés and his conquistadors to overthrow the Aztec Empire. Mexico became a colonial treasure chest, supplying the world's gold and silver. European influences can be seen today in all areas of architecture and design. Indian rebellion began with the Mexican War of Independence in 1810, although it wasn't until the ten-year Mexican Revolution of 1910 that European influence was finally usurped, and an Indian population began to reclaim the land.

3 Selling everything you could want and certainly everything you need, stalls like this one in Morelia's Sunday morning street market display a wealth of traditional wares.

4 Underlying Mexican spirituality is a close and open relationship with death. Much Mexican art and imagery expresses this relationship. Skeletons are represented in all walks of life. Papier mâché, clay, and wooden figures—from doctors through to ice-cream sellers—are all portrayed as skeletons. Skulls even grin from iced biscuits in the bakery. The underlying philosophy is to laugh at, but also to respect, the inevitable human end—death.

5 Configurations of patterned tiles covering large surface areas have become synonymous with Mexican style. They are a specialty that nowadays are exported all over the world.

3

This ideology spilled over into the arts, marking the beginning of the Cultural Revolution. The 1920s saw a cultural renaissance with artists looking back to pre-Hispanic times for inspiration. Artists such as Frida Kahlo and Diego Rivera led the cultural movement, and after years of domination, Mexico began to define an independent image. Spearheading the movement in the architectural world was Luis Barragán. He saw Mexico as an architectural and cultural melting pot, incorporating both pre-Hispanic and colonial influences in his now world-famous architecture.

The photography for this book is guided by this history, but also by the craftspeople and designers who are as passionate about preserving Mexico's cultural history as they are about progressing the modern Mexican style. Architects such as José de Yturbe opened their doors in Mexico City, while in Guanajuato, the famous potter Gorky González unfolded the story of ceramics. The colonial havens of San Miguel de Allende, Querétaro, and Morelia provided a wealth of interior and exterior styles. In contrast, the city of Oaxaca to the south is a colorful fusion of ancient and modern styles. The surrounding villages produce some of the most exquisite traditional textile art, ancient designs intact. Further south, the tiny colonial town of San Cristóbal de las Casas remains the cultural heart of traditional Indian art, and so is one of the most important sources of Mexican style. Here, as in Oaxaca, Indians weave traditional rugs and garments as they have done for centuries.

It is through the work of artists, architects, sculptors, potters, and weavers, whose creativity ties history, religion, the land, and its people together, that we can recognize and reach a true appreciation of Mexican style.

color

Look up and see an azure sky; look down and see ocher dust and peeling walls—the patina of pink blush beneath marigold yellow. The glimpse of a turquoise shawl embroidered with purple birds through a street market shimmering with giant blue and silver balloons and rainbow colored hammocks thrills our visual sense. Mexico celebrates color.

And the legacy is long. The ancient cities of the Aztecs, Maya, Toltecs, and Zapotecs all glowed with color. Today's dusty brown pyramids were once majestic in bold red ocher. Walls and ceilings were covered in murals and frescoes of bright greens, burnt oranges, yellows, and turquoises.

In Aztec society, green was highly prized: jade and the brilliant green feathers of the Quetzal birds were among their most treasured objects. The conquering conquistadors were quick to learn this, exchanging "worthless" tiny green glass beads for Mexican gold.

Hundreds of years on, every color is honored. A stucco wall painted cerise enriches a humble home; lime and yellow taxis in the boulevards of Mexico City brighten the urban sprawl. Color, the silent language, communicates the essence of the Mexican spirit at a single glance.

1 Across the colored domes of San Miguel de Allende in the state of Guanajuato, stands the famous La Parroquia church. It was rebuilt in the last century by a self-taught Indian stone mason, who is said to have communicated his design to builders by drawing his plans in the sand with a stick.

pink

Pink, or *rosa mexicana*, is widely used in Mexico today, but it took the passion of Mexico's most famous architect to put pink firmly on the palette. Luis Barragán became well known in the 1930s for using pink, yellow, and blue in large expanses. He used bright colors to redefine space, and create what he called "magic and surprise" in his work.

2

3

4

1 Designed by Luis Barragán in 1967, San Cristóbal is a ranch for breeding thoroughbred race horses. One hour's drive from Mexico City, the complex includes a family house, swimming pool, and stables—and a dominating use of *rosa mexicana*.

2 No sight is more welcome on a hot Mexico day than the ice-cream man. In Oaxaca, he travels by bicycle, so that he can set up shop on any street corner.

3 Pink details. Pink-purple blooms spill from an earthenware pot against a pale pink wall.

4 From *jugos* (juice) to tacos, you can buy just about anything on street corners throughout Mexico. This girl is selling monkey nuts.

5 A shop front painted pink grabs the attention along a street in San Cristóbal de las Casas. This magical colonial town in the mountains of Chiapas may look sleepy, but in 1994, it hit the headlines when the Zapatista National Liberation Army (representing Mexico's oppressed Indian population) seized the town, rebelling against government policies.

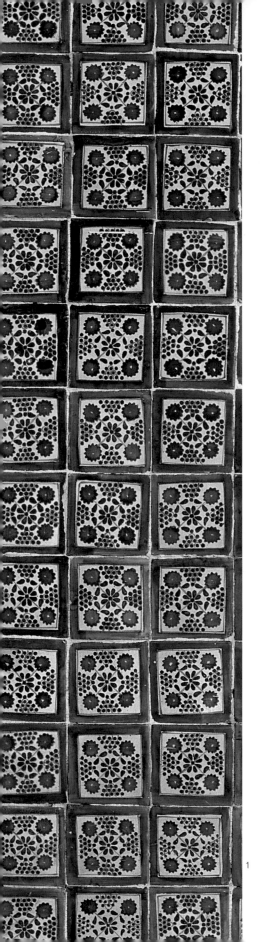

blue

"The sky is a true facade of a house." Luis Barragán

From early morning, as the sun rises, the Mexico sky is sapphire. By afternoon, as the shutters are closing for siesta, it's electric blue. At the day's end, a deep lapis lazuli heralds the night. So many shades of blue—and each one encountered by simply looking...up.

Blue is Mexico's mystical color. Thousands of years ago, it was used to ward off evil spirits. And it's still providing mysteries in our time. Blue is a color to have survived the ravages of time on stone sculptures and scriptures. Referred to today as Mayan blue, scientists have no idea how or from what it was made.

1 Deep ocean blue, and a crisp white. The Mexicans are fond of using tiles to decorate large expanses of wall, both indoors and out. The technique of tin-glazing to produce the tiles is known as *talavera*, after the Spanish town of Talavera de la Reina, where the practice originated.

2 The blue and white partnership orginates from the arrival of the Spanish, who were themselves influenced by Moorish design. This roof top, with a small bell tower atop a domed roof, in Playa del Carmen is a classic example.

1

3 Blue and white patterned bowls from a restaurant in the cosmopolitan Coyoácan district of Mexico City.

4 Water fountains, such as this one in Sierra Nevada, are only ever a stroll away. This blue and white zigzag pattern is commonly used in association with water.

5 Oaxaca, 900 miles south of Mexico City, is a city which reflects a fusion of ancient and modern styles. Its many plaster walls are in untold hues, and none more prevalent than bright blue.

yellow

From the citric brilliance of lemon yellow to the deeper golden tones of marigold, yellow plays a strong role in the decorative scheme of Mexico. Combining effortlessly with other earthy hues, it is an obvious choice for interiors adorned with wooden furniture and simple pottery. Symbolically associated with the sun, it has been a color favored by the Mexicans for centuries. Ancient cultures worshipped the sun as one of their most powerful gods. Today, even lowly household items such as buckets, brushes, and cloths are treated to this revitalizing color.

1 The earthy color combination of a terra-cotta pot against a deep yellow wall.

2 Amid the color of this market in Mexico City, yellow details abound. On this stall selling household products, scouring pads are given the vibrant color treatment.

3 A reel of yellow yarn used for traditional weaving. The brighter, more exaggerated colors of woven textiles are achieved with synthetic (aniline) dyes, adopted through trade with Europe.

4 This ceramic painted lady greets all from her balcony in Oaxaca. Wearing traditional embroidered clothing, she illustrates the method used for carrying goods, by balancing a basket on her head.

5 Candles are an important feature in both fiestas and the celebration of saints' days. Rarely a week goes by without a religious celebration taking place. Lighting candles is always part of the ritual.

6 Yellow injects life into this room of Casa Na Bolom in San Cristóbal de las Casas. It is the perfect color to complement the wooden, colonial-style furniture characterized by the huge oak dining table. Tables such as these were designed to seat up to thirty people.

red

With warrior-like reputations and bloodthirsty rituals, it could be said that the Mesoamericans had a fascination for all things red. Certainly they indulged in bloodletting rituals and human sacrifice to appease the gods.

But these blood-red connections aside, it seems that red was a color dominating the sculptures and structures of ancient times. It was (and still is in some parts of Mexico) made from the *cochineal* bug. First fattening the insect on the nopal cactus, the bugs are crushed, releasing a red juice. Then they are sun-dried or toasted, ground into a powder, and mixed with alum, lime juice, and salt ready for dying.

Another traditional process of creating red dye is called *almagré*. A good example of this is at the hacienda La Laja, (see page 100), where exterior stone walls have been painted in a bright red pigment created by mixing the local red clay with oil.

1 Red is a color theme continued in the dining room of La Laja hacienda, near Querétaro. Renovated originally by architect, Juan Sordo Madaleno, and more recently by José de Yturbe, the style of La Laja is simple, using color as an important architectural tool.

2 Candles against a red wall—a simple but dramatic accent in the home of architect and town planner, José Luis Cortez, in the San Ángel district of Mexico City.

3 A built-in display shelf decorates the wall of the dining room of La Laja. The Mexicans like to make displays of toys and ornaments on shelves such as these. Here, the Mexican flair for color combination is perfectly illustrated, in a confident show of pink and red.

naturals

What better way to offset bright colors than with nature's own. Wood, clay, stone, and marble are all provided by the sun and the earth, and make serene backdrops against which to pitch more vibrant shades.

And least you think that neutrals are not typically Mexican, it is worth noting that Toltec storehouses were said to be brimming with shells, timber, and flaxwork, and the huge stone walls of royal palaces were made from river rocks. In the city of Tenochtitlán, these rocks were so revered, they employed individuals to polish and care for the stonework.

These natural materials and their hues are still much loved in Mexico today.

1 A grid of paving slabs and pebbles dominates the courtyard of a house in Valle de Brava, just outside Mexico City. Designed by José de Yturbe, the use of stones and pebbles is a common feature of his work.

2 Copperware on display at the Villa Montana Hotel, in Morelia. Hand-worked copper is a prominent craft, most particularly in the town of Santa Clara del Cobre in Michoacán.

3 Towering bamboo baskets from a market in Mexico City. Woven baskets are usually made from cane, rush, or palm leaf strips.

4 Earthy tones dominate at the workshop of potter Gorky González. Living in the hillside city of Guanajuato, a city known for its cultural and artistic vibrancy, he is one of Mexico's most well-known potters.

white

"We saw in those cities Cues and oratories like towers and fortresses and all gleaming white, and it was a wonderful thing to behold." Bernal Díaz del Castillo. This is the first-hand account of a conquistador, as he entered the Aztec city of Tenochtitlán. Today, white is still a popular color, used as a whitewash for the interior and exterior of buildings, and for furniture and furnishings.

White is the quintessential canvas, an obvious start point, and a cool, calm influence in a country so dominated by color. For example, white cotton for women's dresses and *huipil* (tunics) is the perfect canvas for the rich embroidery that adorns them.

For dramatic effect, brilliant white makes an eye-catching contrast to vivid walls, and a striking partner for natural materials such as black volcanic stone.

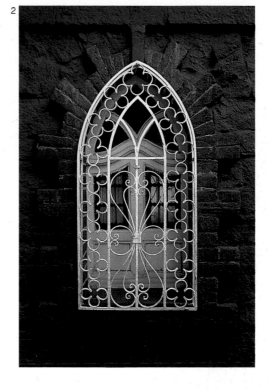

1 Over the terra-cotta roof tops of San Cristóbal de las Casas, in Chaipas, white churches gleam in the valley. This colonial hillside town is renowned for its charming white-washed houses.

2 White is used as an accent on the outside of houses. On the window of this house in Mexico City, wrought iron grillwork has been painted white to accentuate the flowing design. The arched window is typical of colonial style.

3 Although weaving and embroidery are traditionally a woman's art, some woven textiles, such as this white bed spread from Morelia are made by men on a treadle loom.

4 Many items of dress have ornate decorative borders around collars and hemlines. Here, the use of a single color makes a bold statement against the white fabric.

5 This detail of a shell and plaster wall is the exterior of a 3-foot-high play house, built especially for children. It stands in the garden of an artist's house in San Miguel de Allende.

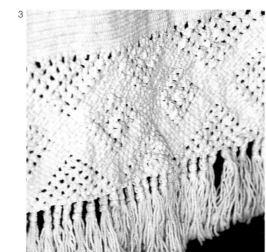

multi-colors

1 *Hamaca* (hammocks) are sold everywhere, but are a specialty from the villages of Mitla and Juchitán in Oaxaca state. They were once woven from the finest silk: these days it's usually cotton or nylon.

2 Viva Mexico! Tiny fiesta hats sold for Día de la Independencia. Celebrated on September 15, thousands of people gather in Mexico City's *Zócalo* (city square) to hear the president recite from the famous call to gather arms and rebel against the Spanish in 1810.

3 Hand-carved and painted toss-toys in Morelia.

4 Reindeer are given the rainbow treatment. Materials such as cotton and raffia are woven and twisted into animals to sell at the market.

5 Multi-colored cotton mats. Natural dyes are still used to color yarn, but synthetic dyes are more common.

Nature reveals wonderful color combinations—the fiery red chili with a green stalk, coconut brown with bright white, or watermelon pink with an accent of dark brown pips—nature has no

rules for color combinations. The Mexicans have a natural flair for color combining, from unusual pairings using colors from different ends of the spectrum, to a whole vibrant medley. Nowhere is this more apparent than in the fiesta. Festivals are commonplace, with villages celebrating a particular saint or pre-colonial rain god. On fiesta days, the streets are filled with an explosion of color in costumes and processions, papier mâché statues, banners, and games.

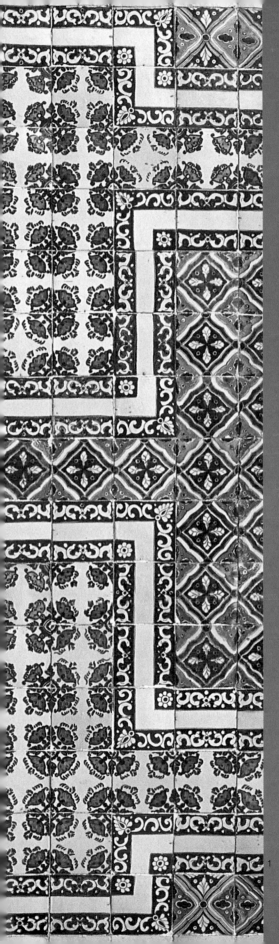

pattern

"Art is the only legacy that lasts." Octavio Paz
Whether woven into cloth or painted onto a cave wall, humankind has always created patterns to communicate. Whatever the culture, whatever the canvas, these patterns hold the key to civilizations now passed, making the artistic creation not just an object of beauty, but a historic tale, revealing all that has gone.

On February 10, 1519, Captain Hernan Cortés and his fleet arrived in the Gulf of Mexico from Spain. In a powerful message of intended permanency, he burned all eleven ships before marching on to the Aztec capital of Tenochtitlán. Conquistador Bernal Díaz was mesmerized by the sophisticated city, writing in his journal: *"gazing on such wonderful sights, we did not know what to say, or whether what appeared before us was real."*

So much was lost in the subsequent conquest and oppression. Franciscan missionaries were sent over to convert the population to Christianity, but many beliefs and rituals did survive and the patterns and motifs that illustrate those beliefs still exist today.

Mexican art is a testament to that history, with patterns revealing how the layers of Mexico's unique past and the fusion of cultural styles has created beautiful and new forms of expression.

1 A detail of the intricate tile work of Casa de los Azulejos (House of Tiles) in Mexico City. Although the patterns and style of the eighteenth-century tiles are typically Spanish, they were produced in China and shipped back to Mexico to adorn this house that at one time was the residence of the Counts of Orizaba.

florals

Mexico is a floral extravaganza. Bougainvillea, marigolds, and purple cockscombe overflow at street markets and in terra-cotta pots along the sidewalk. Country roads bob with color, as enormous bunches are tied to people's backs as they make the journey from village to town.

Flowers hold a special place in Mexican art. Huge blooms are embroidered onto clothing, painted onto plates, and carved into stone. In the work of ancient cultures, a simple four-petal symbol was a favorite for jewelry, while royalty were often pictured carrying posies.

Flowers were also used as offerings. Quetzalcoatl, the Aztec feathered serpent deity encouraged the sacrifice of flowers instead of flesh. The marigold in particular was a powerful symbol. Marigolds were given as offerings to the dead, a tradition that continues in the celebrations of the Day of the Dead, when the flower decorates cemeteries and home altars, and trails of its golden petals are scattered so that the dead can find their way home.

1 Oaxacan woman wearing a *rebozo* (shawl) lavishly embroidered with floral blooms. She sits with similarly embroidered textiles around her for people to buy.

2 The costume of Zapotec society is a highly decorative dress, adorned with incredible rich blooms that are sewn in a simple satin stitch.

3 Floral prints cover rolls of decorative papers. Papers such as these are often used to line the inner lids of storage chests. Other mementos, such as photographs and religious images are fixed on top to make the boxes truly personal and special.

4 The Mexicans relish the art of display. On the fruit stall, pieces of fruit and vegetables are cut into shapes ready for eating, and displayed on a floral printed plastic table cloth.

geometric

Not surprisingly, perhaps, geometric shapes are most prevalent in architecture—particularly ancient architecture. Take the pyramid—four sides, stepped, and always with a staircase. It was here, perhaps, that the fascination with geometric patterns began.

The Spanish arrival brought new artistic skills, none more important than *talavera* (the art of glazed and fired ceramics). Talavera de la Reina was the Spanish center for this method of tile-making, but it eventually became a generic term for the practice of blue and white tiling that was a popular tradition in sixteenth-century Spain. The combination of the two colors lends itself to a wealth of geometric patterns that decorate the exterior of many structures, from roof tops down to garden fountains.

◁ 1   2

1 The strong sculptural shape of a stone staircase is decorated in the traditional *talavera* style at the Sierra Nevada hotel in San Miguel de Allende. The use of dynamic geometric pattern is extended to the geranium pots.

2 Zapotec design, of the indigenous people of Oaxaca State. Certain villages in this area are famed for their traditional woven textiles. This detail is from a design that was produced in the hillside village of Teotitlán del Valle.

3 Talavera geometry from a domed church in Querétaro. This city, just north of Mexico City, is characterized by its colonial architecture.

stonework

1 The Pyramid of the Sun in Teotihuacán is Mesoamerica's largest ruin, looming 195 feet from the dust. Translated the word means "Place where God was Created." At the time of its prime (A.D. 500) it was one of of the world's largest cities.

2 Patterned brick formation from Teotihuacán. The ancient ruins lie about 27 miles from Mexico City.

3 Precise brickwork patterns from a wall in the San Ángel district of Mexico City.

4 Intricate stonework from the ruins of Mitla, a Zapotec city just outside Oaxaca, that dates from A.D. 100. This is an interior facade of a temple room. Architects and sculptors used the movement of the sun to play visual tricks. Many carvings were tilted outwards, so that when the sun cast its shadow, the facade would appear to be in even greater relief.

5 The remnants of the massive stone structures of Mexico's pre-colonial past have had great influence on today's architects, who combine stone paving and cobbles to create their own patterns for courtyard and interior surfaces.

More than a visual and textural treat, stonework pattern has a mathematical precision that provides structural strength, keeping walls upright, and pyramids earthquake proof for hundreds of years.

Stone sculpture is more fluid than stone patterns, but no less expressive. Thousand-year-old sculptures can teach us much about ancient rituals and customs. Some Olmec stonework (from 1200 B.C.) features humans in various stages of transformation into animals, while others show religious festivals, where humans would impersonate gods before they were sacrificed and their skin flayed for other men to wear.

6

7

6 Stone carving of a woman at Casa Chata de Tlalpan in Mexico City. The niche and statue is carved into the garden wall.

7 Miniature stone statuettes were carved in abundance for household shrines. From birth to death, there was a god for every facet of life in the Mesoamerican pantheon.

8

8 Although sculptures reveal much about the past, ancient figures also create many new and unanswered questions. Many stone carvings were buried with ancient royalty to guide them into the afterlife, and some Olmec figures (the oldest known civilization in Mexico, dating from 3000 B.C.) buried stone statues in a strange but detailed tableaux form, yet archeologists have no idea what this represents.

9 Weathered stone figures, said to look after souls sent to purgatory, stand in the garden of Casa Prieto, in Mexico City.

natural motifs

Nature was worshipped by the ancient cultures of Mesoamerica, and many rituals and beliefs were based on the concept of harmony and balance on earth. Legends involved animals: The rabbit was held as the symbol of the moon; the owl, as a symbol of night and the underworld. In fact, the Mayan and Aztec calendars had strong associations with natural phenomena. Each day was devoted to either an animal—jaguar, eagle, or monkey, or the natural world—wind, water, or the sun.

This deep fascination with the natural world has passed down to today's artists, designers, and potters. Butterflies, fish, big cats, and snakes all feature in their work. Their exuberant creativity even extends to flora, and native fruits such as pineapples, oranges, and melons, which appear in paintings, food sculptures, and ceramic designs.

1 Flowers were special motifs for the ancient Mexicans, who used them throughout their art. Many goddesses were depicted wearing flowers like these on their heads. This is a detail from an embroidered dress.

2 The use of natural motifs also relates to the journey of the soul into the afterlife. The manner of a person's death had more influence on their afterlife than the good they had done during their lifetime. The Aztecs believed that those who died a noble death—warriors in battle, women in childbirth—were transformed into a hummingbird or a butterfly, flitting in the warmth of the Mexico sun.

3 A pattern of fish decorates the surface of a highly glazed terra-cotta plate made in one of the local *Alfarerria* (craft workshops) near Morelia.

4 Real fruits make wonderful natural sculptures, like these apples fixed into pyramids and displayed in blue and white vessels in a house in Valle de Brava, designed by José de Yturbe.

5 Edible art? Colorful papier mâché fruit pieces and a fruit cocktail painting in a house designed by Luis Barragán in Mexico City.

6 Tiled garden table with an eclectic collection of natural motifs—chilis, pears, and flowers—from the Villa Montana hotel in Morelia.

7 Ceramic pineapple, also from the Villa Montana. Nestling in the Santa Maria hills, just 5 minutes from the heart of Morelia, the rooms of this splendid hotel comprise antiques, regional handcrafts, and folk art.

1

religious

Mexicans are a deeply spiritual people. Hidden within the themes and symbols of Catholicism lie the threads of pre-Hispanic belief. Catholicism has been accepted—but on their terms. Rain gods can be found buried beneath a cross; churches act as a meeting point for performing ancient rituals.

The idea of containing religion within a Sunday church service is completely at odds with their way of life. Everyday, at every moment, evidence of this is apparent. From a little altar shelf with a wooden cross sitting above the donkey in the barn to a skeleton hanging from a taxi driver's mirror—these are all artistic details of spiritual thought.

Every home has an altar, lovingly decorated with treasured objects, paper flowers, and crosses. These are the focus of prayer and meditation. Religious icons are everywhere, but none is more apparent than the Madonna of Guadalupe. With her dark skin and blue robes, she is the Mexican manifestation of the Virgin Mary, and a vital link between Catholicism and Indian spirituality. Guadalupe's image first appeared to an Indian on a hill outside Mexico City not far from where the Aztec gods were once worshipped.

1 *Retablos* (small religious paintings) decorate the wall of a room in Casa Liza (now a bed and breakfast) in San Miguel de Allende. These paintings are usually executed on tin, and give thanks to a saint for an answered prayer.

2 With Christianity so much a part of daily life, religious icons and paintings are commonplace in Mexican interiors. Here, wooden cherubs grace the wall of Casa Beryl, a house designed by José de Yturbe just outside Mexico City.

3 Religious imagery is ubiquitous. Portraits of Jesus and prominent saints are sold on postcards at street markets. Note the image of the Madonna of Guadalupe, patroness saint of Mexico, on the middle left of the picture.

day of the dead

"The word death is not pronounced in New York, in Paris, in London, because it burns the lips. The Mexican, in contrast, is familiar with death, jokes about it, caresses it, sleeps with it, celebrates it; it is one of his favorite toys and his most steadfast love." Octavio Paz

Every year in Mexico an invitation is sent to the dead. They are welcomed back to indulge in earthly pleasures in a celebration known as Day of the Dead. This festival, which is throught to be Aztec in origin, lasts for several days. Homes and cemeteries are decorated with ornamental skulls and skeletons, some are made from marigolds, others are dressed in elaborate costume.

1 Preparation for the Day of the Dead can begin months in advance. Casa de las Artesanías, the Sunday market in Morelia, hangs skeletons amidst the ceramic work.

2 The first night of the fiesta on October 27 is for spirits who have no living relatives. Jugs of water and chunks of bread are offered to the dead on street corners. The next day is for the souls who have died violently. Food and drink are offered outside the home to hold malevolent spirits at bay. On the night of October 31, dead children come home to play. The home altar becomes the focus, decorated with lighted candles, food, and a treasured toy. The day of the Faithful Dead on November 1 is for adults who have died most recently, and for remembering family ancestors. At twilight, the community moves to the cemetery for an all-night conversation with the dead. By the evening of November 2, the dead are encouraged to return to the afterlife.

3 Laughing at death. The message is clear and simple: mock death, for it is a part of life you cannot escape.

4 The idea of dressing skeletons in colonial clothes is attributed to Mexico's most famous pre-revolutionary engraver, José Guadalupe Posada. Nowadays every profession, from secretary to nut seller, is portrayed in skeleton form.

5 A skeleton surrounded by the tree of death—symbolizing the human condition. Decoration such as this is on display all year round.

texture
and materials

Texture has always added a sense of drama and surprise to architecture, art, and design. Aztec palaces would feature one wall in layered gold leaf, while another would be built entirely of giant rocks. Spanish-style cathedrals used gold and rich oil paints on ornately carved wood and enormous ridged columns to create the illusion of godliness.

In fabric work, too, natural fibers provide a colorful textural language. Enormous Aztec tapestries were elaborately stitched with green quetzal feathers, and today, traditional *huipils* and *rebozos* are textured with embroidered floral blooms. The use of diverse surfaces and materials is an important feature of Mexican style.

Modern architects use texture to define and shape space. Luis Barragán employed materials favored by pre-Hispanic builders in an effort to contrast textures. The following generation of architects, such as Javier Sordo Madaleno, expanded on this usage. Madaleno has been known to use thick, industrial steel coil to line walls, while his contemporary, José de Yturbe, creates dramatic contrast with large expanses of chipped stone floors, alongside smooth terra-cotta tiles.

1 A miniature model of a typical Mexican market stall. It shows the depth of attention to presentation shown by stall owners in their display of myriad wares.

tiles

Azulejos (tin glazed tiles) have a mixed cultural background. The technique arrived in Mexico with the Spanish, who had learned the skill from the Moors. Their teachers, the Persians, in turn, had discovered it from the Chinese.

Pottery was a well-established industry by the sixteenth century, but the Aztecs were fascinated by the beautiful Spanish tiles, and the technique that created such bright, shiny glazes. They embraced the new skills—giving a fresh twist to the Spanish style by decorating the tiles with Aztec images and rich colors. The tin-glazing technique (known as *talavera*, after the town specializing in this process in Spain) involves covering the clay in a tin mixture and firing it at moderate heat. Once cooled, the tiles are painted with colorful patterns, then fired again at great heat.

Today, *azulejos* are exported all over the world, and in Mexico they brighten up any surface, from the dome of a Catholic church to the bottom of a swimming pool.

1 The city of Puebla has the highest concentration of tiled facades and interiors. Talavera potters settled there from Spain, and so it became the prominent center for tile manufacture. Over time the use and practice has spread throughout Mexico. Here they decorate the area above a fountain in Oaxaca.

2 The beauty of tin-glazed tiles lies in their handmade, bright colors and shiny finish, created by the special "double-firing" technique.

3 Use of decorative tiles extends to all surfaces. Here a line of modern tiles is inlaid into a terra-cotta tiled table top.

4 This stone staircase in a colonial house in San Cristóbal de las Casas shows tiles complementing a strong use of color. The rich earthy hue of terra-cotta blends perfectly with the wooden balustrade and orange walls. Vivid contrast is provided by the blue and white tiles decorating the side of the staircase.

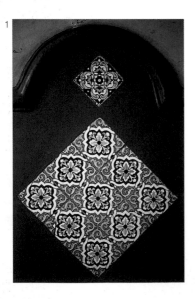

4 ▷

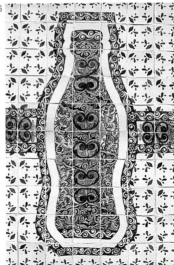

5, 6

5 This colonial-style kitchen in Casa Liza in San Miguel de Allende has smooth-tiled surfaces throughout. The design is based on an original seen in the Franz Mayer museum in Mexico City. Mayer was a German immigrant who collected an extensive collection of colonial arts and crafts during the late nineteenth century.

6 Patterned tiles are arranged to create further shape and pattern, such as this Coca-Cola bottle from a shop front in San Cristóbal de las Casas in Chiapas.

7 Because of their shiny glaze, tiles brighten up otherwise clinical surfaces in kitchens and bathrooms, like this example in Casa Azul, in San Miguel de Allende.

8 Intricate patterns from a tiled facade in San Cristóbal de las Casas. Even though the pattern is symmetrical, each tile was individually hand painted, so tiny imperfections become apparent.

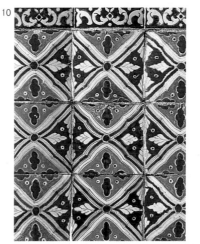

9 In the kitchen in Casa Lisa, the surface of the traditional oven with its sunken hot plates and the backsplash area are covered in beautiful decorative tiles.

10 A section of tilework from the famous Casa de los Azulejos (House of Tiles) in Mexico City. The house was built in 1596, although the tiles adorning the exterior date from the eighteenth century.

wood

Woodcarvers, with their tendency to decorate any available surface were already very adept by the time of the Spanish conquest. Woods such as ebony, mahogany, rosewood, and *sabino* or Spanish cedar became popular during colonial times for everything from carved headboards to enormous tables. As Spanish trade developed, new skills were absorbed from around the world, such as Chinese marquetry and lacquerware. Twentieth-century designers use wood in a sculptural way: thick chunks make simple tables, seats and shelves.

1 Wood warms the dining room of Hacienda Laleta, outside San Miguel de Allende. The wooden-framed arched windows, typical of colonial architecture, are complemented by the hacienda-sized table and chairs, seating eight.

2 Sit down and you are wearing a feathered headdress. This ornate carved wooden chair, inspired by pre-Hispanic design, is from Casas de las Artesanías in Morelia, which is devoted to the display and retail of local Michoachán crafts.

3 A dining table is crafted from individual squares of wood in the nineteenth-century rustic style. It beautifully highlights the grain in the wood, creating a wonderful textural surface.

4 Some of the finest woodworking skills can still be seen in hand-carved sculptural work, such as the intricate, brightly painted toys and animals of Oaxaca. These colorful wooden *juguetes* (folk toys) are referred to as "the fiesta of the object" by writer Octavio Paz.

5 Wooden combs with a national spirit. These are from a stall outside the *Zocálo* in Mexico City, sold on Día de la Independencia, a festival celebrating rebellion against the Spanish. Combs are not just produced for personal use; small wooden combs are used by weavers to hold the warp and weft threads in place as they create their patterns.

6 Carved wooden whisks for whipping hot chocolate are a must-have for every Mexican kitchen. The drinking of hot chocolate has an illustrious history. Cocoa beans were once used as currency in Mexico—hence only the very rich could afford to drink their wealth.

metal

"A sun all of gold...and a moon all of silver...I saw among them wonderful works of art, and I marveled at the subtle genius of men in distant lands." German artist, Albrecht Dürer, wrote this after seeing the many works of art shipped from Mexico to Europe at the beginning of colonization.

The metalwork techniques of the pre-Hispanic cultures were highly advanced. They could weld silver to gold; inlay gold into copper; and hand-beat metals into sheets that were paper-thin. Copper artifacts and iron tools were produced, but metal craft was dominated by jewelry. The Spanish introduced new techniques, including popular filigree work, where tiny threads of metal are strung together to create fine jewelry.

5

1 Miniature *milagros* (miracles) are made as offerings of prayer or special thanks to a particular saint. Made from poor quality silver, then painted gold, they usually take the form of arms, legs, animals, humans, and hearts.

2 Copper pots from Casa de las Artesanías in Morelia. The copper is heated in a *fragua* (traditional oven), then beaten into shape by hand.

3 Under lock and key. This chest with its ornate colonial style iron lock is from Hacienda La Laja, outside the town of Querétaro.

4 A metal door knocker takes the figurative form of a man wearing a feathered headdress.

5 A door bell, oxidized with age, and dating from 1810 hangs before the front entrance to Casa Chata de Tlalpan in Mexico City.

silver

Silver was considered a mystical object to the pre-Hispanic cultures. It was thought to have dropped from the moon, whereas gold was thought to have been a metal of the gods, dropped from the sun. Silvercasting at that time used a special technique known as the "lost-wax" method. The molds were made by creating shapes from a mixture of charcoal and clay, then covered in wax and another layer of clay. This was pierced at the bottom and baked. The wax melted and leaked through the hole revealing the cast. Molten silver was poured into the mold and when it had hardened and cooled, the mold was broken and the silver polished.

When the Spanish arrived, they couldn't believe the amount of silver and gold lying buried in the Mexican earth, nor the elaborate workmanship of the locals. They began to plunder the silver resources at La Valenciana outside Guanajuato, and at Taxco near Mexico City. At one stage the mines of Guanajuato supplied one third of all the world's silver, making Mexico a colonial treasure chest.

During this time, Indian artisans were banned from using or possessing precious metals. Today, ancient jewelry designs and techniques have been revived, and silver work continues to be one of Mexico's biggest exports.

1

1 Silver seashells from Casa Beryl, a house just outside Mexico City. The majority of Mexico's silver now comes from the town of Taxco, where there are regular silver fairs.

2 A cross decorated with silver *milagros* (miracles) from the Villa Montana, Morelia. *Milagros* include metal body parts, hearts, and heads made of low grade silver. They give thanks to a favorite saint.

3 Silver by candlelight. These handmade candleholders are from Morelia.

4 A silver brooch engraved with the Aztec calendar. This was a 260-day calendar: a cycle of 20 days was continually repeated. Each day had a different association, usually an animal such as a monkey, deer, or dog, or natural phenomena, such as an earthquake or rainfall.

stone

The architects of today have created a renaissance of pre-Hispanic style, symbolized, among other things, by their passion for building in stone. South of Mexico City lies a black volcanic wasteland known as El Pedregal (Stony Place). It has become a favored source of rock used by many modern architects for floors and steps. Another characteristic material is river rocks—large, smooth boulders. These rocks were used for building whole walls in ancient palaces: they were often transported long distances overland to reach their destination. Together with stone tiles and pebbles, these materials are a familiar sight in modern Mexican interiors.

1 Volcanic stone tiles for the floor and steps of Casa Prieto, a house designed by Luis Barragán. The colored *pulquería* balls displayed in a carved stone basin date from the nineteenth century.

2 Large stone slabs make a striking coffee table, complementing a predominantly stone interior.

3 Stone used in great, sleek expanses, as in José de Yturbe's house in Mexico City. This is the main entrance, with a door fashioned entirely from black volcanic stone.

3 ▷

fibers

Mexican crafts people twist, knot, and weave a multitude of fibers into textiles and objects. From rushes and reeds, to yarn, and plastic string and rope, they can work all these materials into objects of great strength and versatility.

Historically, fibers were dyed using combinations of plants, flowers, bark, and even sea snails. An ancient recipe for yellow includes 8½ pounds of the carcuma root mixed with the juice of 80 or 90 limes. These days, synthetic dyes are replacing natural ones, yet some weaving communities, particularly in Oaxaca State, are determined to retain their use.

1 Sombreros are essential headwear for anyone working out in the hot Mexican sun. They are sold piled high at every market.

2 Hanks of homespun hand-dyed wool on sale in Teotitlán, in the state of Oaxaca. Traditionally, natural dyes are made from flowers, bark, leaves, fruits, and insects, such as the cochineal bug.

3 The ubiquitous woven plastic bag—always to be seen on market stalls. The diamond pattern is very similar to the traditional geometric patterns found on the woven rugs and shawls of the Zapotec weavers.

4 Coarse fibers of homespun and hand-colored yarn ready to be woven into rugs or blankets.

5 Mexicans can utilize all sorts of materials to create decorative objects. Colored plastic rope is used to make bags and mats.

6 Wools are woven into clothes, shawls, rugs, and mats using patterns from pre-Hispanic times. Many of the symbols represent myths and legends. For example, in Chiapas, a diamond represents the Mayan universe. They believed the earth was a cube, and the sky had four corners.

7 Cheerful knitted ladies on a market stall.

8 Artifacts made from grasses and canes complement a natural interior, such as these maize leaf fans. They create textural variety against the rough-hewn wooden table.

9 Twisted palm fronds are tied to the front of houses to keep away evil spirits. This woven talisman is from a house in San Miguel de Allende.

10 Large, flat, woven maize fan used for controlling the fire and fanning the smoke.

11 Raffia mask from Morelia's Sunday street market. Masks were worn in pre-Hispanic times during dances and shamanistic rituals. Nowadays, many of them mix ancient styles with Catholic and Spanish imagery.

textiles

Textiles are steeped in tradition. The vocabulary of the bright embroidered designs stitched onto female garments identify tribe, age, and whether the wearer is single or married.

The famous Mexican artist, Frida Kahlo, wore nothing but traditional textiles: the *huipil* (tunic) and *enredo* (skirt), tied with a brightly colored *faja* (sash).

The basic Indian loom for woven textiles was developed hundreds of years before the Spanish arrived, and is still in use today. Known as the back-strap, it is fixed between a tree and the weaver's back. The Spanish introduced the treadle loom, operated by a foot pedal, which makes larger pieces of cloth.

1 Embroidery has its roots in pre-Hispanic myth, using images and symbols from the legends of the past. These *huipils* are from the villages around Oaxaca. The clothes are not tailored, but tied with strips of brightly colored cotton.

2 A stitch in time: a woman at work in Casa de las Artesanías in Morelia, where crafts people demonstrate their work as well as sell their handcrafted products. The intricate cross-stitch pattern is considered to be one of the most labor intensive of embroidery techniques.

3 A woman from Oaxaca weaving a Zapotec design. Depending on the size of a rug, the whole family may help out with making it.

4 Woven rug of Zapotec design from Oaxaca. In pre-Hispanic times, cotton, feathers, and rabbit fur were woven into rugs, then the Spanish introduced wool. Since the 1960s, synthetic fibers such as rayon and acrylic have been used in place of wool, which are not as long lasting.

paper

It may be the simplest of materials, but in Mexico, paper is worked into the most delicate and detailed art forms. Every fiesta and special occasion features handmade paper art. *Banderolas*, or cut-paper banners flicker in the streets; papier-mâché dolls swing from lampposts; paper flowers adorn home altars.

Paper-making is an ancient skill made from the bark of two trees—the *morus* (mulberry) for white paper, and the *ficus* (fig) for darker varieties. Traditionally, the bark was scraped and dried by men, while making the paper was women's work. The process begins with washing the bark, then boiling it with ashes. It is then rinsed, laid out and beaten until the fibers knit together, and dried in the sun. The technique was first used for the sacred manuscripts of the Maya.

1–2 Papier-mâché dolls and animals are made in all shapes and sizes and carefully painted. On the dolls above, attention is paid to the makeup and jewelry, with shiny paper fragments providing a glamorous touch.

3 Papier-mâché angel, for the home altar or decoration all year round, combines Christian and Indian charateristics.

4 *Banderolas* are strung from lampposts to walls at fiesta time. Originally, they were used to mark the path, and honor the holy during religious processions. Each one was painstakingly cut out by hand. These days, the artist has a regular production line, making up to 50 at a time.

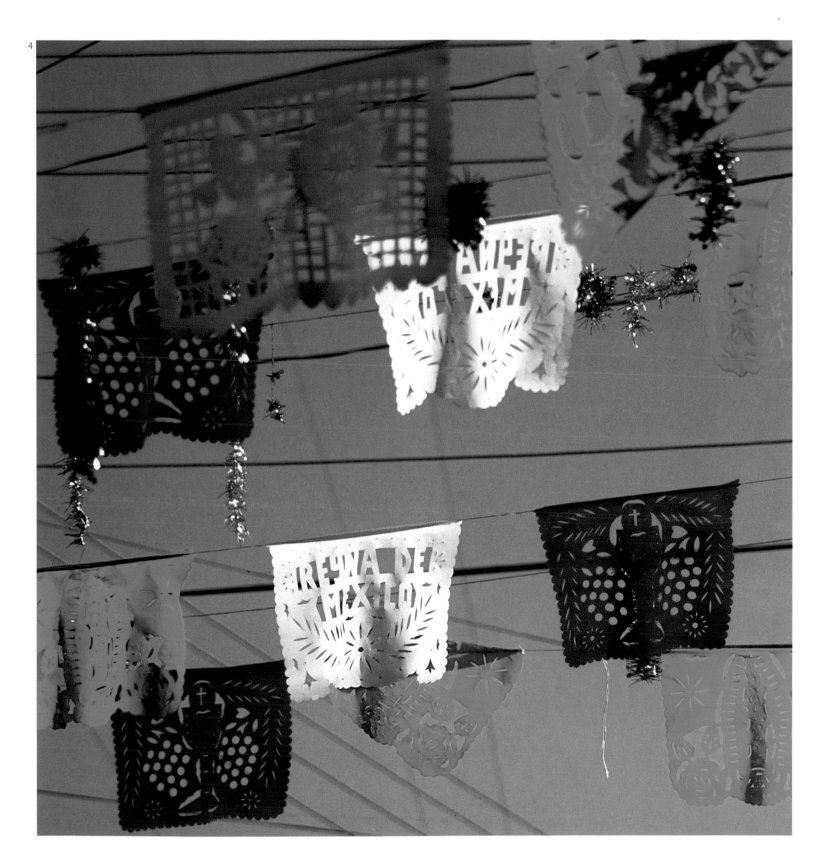

leather

From his trimmed sombrero to his ankle-high boots, the Mexican *charro* (cowboy) dressed in leather from head to toe. With legendary style, he established hide at the heart of Mexican style.

It is leather's resilient nature that allows it to withstand heavy wear and outdoor conditions. It also weathers beautifully, sometimes taking on a more radiant sheen as time passes.

Today, the legend of the cowboy lives on, and leather ware focuses on saddles, belts, and boots. But its application has extended into the home. The durable hide is used for seat covers on the typical *equipale* chairs, and for accessories such as lampshades. It is often embellished with flowing pattern work that is achieved by the labor-intensive method of punching and tooling, and enhanced with dye or varnish.

1 Every Mexican *charro* needs a stitched leather saddle. Saddles became popular with the arrival of the Spanish in the sixteenth century. This one is made from pig hide.

2 Leather trimmed sombrero from San Miguel de Allende—a must for the *hacendado* (hacienda owner).

3 Leather lamp with cross-stitched seams from Casa Prieto, a house designed by Luis Barragán outside Mexico City.

4 The final touch for the *charro*—a hand-stitched leather belt from a stall at the *Zocálo* in Mexico City. Known for their detailed leather accessories, *charros* were a big part of daily life on the hacienda.

◁ 1

4

ceramics

Ceramics were considered one of the highest arts during Aztec times. The technique was said to have been passed down by Quetzalcoatl himself, the serpent god with a feathered headdress. Pottery was made by coiling the clay into a circle and building up the sides of the pot, and then scraping and molding it into shape. It was then painted deep, earthy tones, and fired. The conquering Spanish brought with them the potter's wheel, and special glazing techniques which the Meso-americans absorbed and added to their established tradition.

With its backbone of pre-Hispanic tradition, the ancient art is a symbol of Mexico's history, absorbing styles and techniques from all over the world—Spain, Asia, the Middle East, and most recently the West—making it one of Mexico's most famous and well-established arts.

1

1 Like an unbroken chain, ceramic techniques have been handed down through generations. The work shop of potter Gorky González in Guanajuato, uses the same technique developed 300 years ago. Every piece is wheeled and painted by hand, and the clay is collected locally from the mountains of Santa Rosa.

2 The bulbous form of ceramic water containers along a built-in shelf at the entrance of Casa Beryl, create a dramatic contrast of shape and line against the stone steps. The grouping of large pots was a favorite theme of Luis Barragán, who encouraged the application of local arts and crafts in his work.

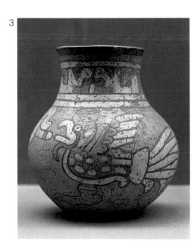

3 An original Mayan ceramic pot, discovered in Chiapas, now in the Museo Nacional de Antropologia. Ancient pottery was mostly colored a deep, earthy red, and adorned with animals and other natural motifs.

4 A collection of *talavera* ceramics from FONART, a center for arts and crafts in Mexico. *Talavera* refers to the brightly colored, shiny glaze, used in Mexico since the arrival of the Spanish.

5 Little ceramic devils riding a cow, made in Puebla, Mexico's pottery capital. The use of devils in Mexican art is common. Although obviously a Catholic image, the concept of bad forces and an arduous underworld has always been a strong theme throughout Mesoamerican ideology.

6 Even meal times are alive with color and pattern. The *talavera* plate is a finished piece from the workshop of Gorky González in Guanajuato.

7 Historically, water sources, such as mountain springs have been worshipped as magic, life-giving places. When the Spanish arrived, fountains became a regular architectural fixture, an influence from the Moors, who enjoyed the concept of communal water. This water jug fountain is in a restaurant, La Sazon, in the Tlalpan district of Mexico City.

architecture

"Mexico rises between two seas like a huge truncated pyramid: its four sides are the four points of the compass, its staircases are the climates of all the zones, and its high plateau is the house of the sun and constellations." Octavio Paz

Intrinsically linked to its expansive landscape, Mexican architecture has an intense relationship with the land. From pyramids to sky scrapers, buildings are—like the landscape—vast. It is about construction on a colossal scale; and it is about space. But architecture is also an illustration of the country's dark and brooding past. Zapotec pyramids, Spanish haciendas, seventeenth-century churches all reveal conquests won and wars lost.

The twentieth century heralded a new age. The end of revolution and civil war from 1910–1920 meant radical cultural change. Mexicans were encouraged by the government and artists alike to explore and understand their own heritage. In the architectural world, this movement was lead by Luis Barragán. He combined elements of the pre-Hispanic ruins with Spanish simplicity. His work marks a turning point in architecture, the beginning of an individual identity, and an understanding of what it means to be Mexican.

1 An ancient staircase leading to a temple at Monte Albán, the Zapotec city in Oaxaca. Stairs are an important architectural symbol, as each step leads you closer to the sky, the birthplace and playing grounds of the gods.

walls

Mexican walls are masters of surprise, and the keepers of secrets. They mirror the contradictory Mexican character: warm and loving to outsiders, with their cheerful colors, yet heavily guarding a privacy with their solid impenetrable surface. The Mexican writer and philosopher, Octavio Paz, explains the Mexican psyche and need for privacy in his famous book, *The Labyrinth of Solitude*: "We hide within ourselves....We oscillate between intimacy and withdrawal, between a shout and a silence, between fiesta and a wake, without ever truly surrendering ourselves."

1 Architect, José de Yturbe plays with light and shadow on the walls of his own house in Mexico City.

2 Layers of life—the crumbling exterior wall of a grocery store in San Cristóbal de las Casas. Buildings receive regular fresh coats of paint, usually in the summer.

3 Street scene of colored stucco houses. The doors often lead straight into a courtyard, while windows on the outside wall are kept to a minimum to avoid tax. This street is in the district of San Ángel in Mexico City.

◁ 1

4 Large walls of color dominate San Cristóbal, the racehorse stables designed by Luis Barragán for the Egerström family in the 1960s. Long walls contain enormous "windows," revealing glimpses of the stables at work.

4

windows

Mexicans have worshipped the sun since civilization began. Consequently, they have a deep understanding of the dramatic interplay between light and shade, and windows have become an architectural feature of this relationship at work. They are designed to let great shafts of light into cool, dark rooms. Covered by shutters, protecting against a searing afternoon sun, they provide a peephole to the outside world, letting in a chink of light. On the coast where a view of the sea is a must, tiny windows called *ventanitas*, are cut into the walls and door of the *palapas*.

1 Windows with a view in Chiluca, a modern suburb in Mexico City.

2 Bars are a dominant characteristic in front of windows that face onto the street.

3–4 Sometimes arched in the colonial style, sometimes square and simple, windows are nearly always accentuated with color.

doors

Over-sized double doors became an established architectural style with the building of colonial churches and haciendas. They were doors for grand scale architecture, and were usually made from solid hardwood, such as mesquite and *sabino* (Spanish cedar)—the thicker the wood the more important the building.

1 With surrounding walls covered in greenery and colonial framework, this door in Casa Lisa, looks as if well-kept secrets hide behind its wooden panels.

2–4 Animals are a favorite for door knockers. The fish is from La Casa de los Perros (the house of dogs), a colonial mansion in San Miguel de Allende. The bull is typical of the hacienda. This one is from La Laja.

The lion is from Morelia, the capital of Michoachán State.

5 Colonial details abound in this doorway—blue and white *azulejos*, and a frame in the Baroque *plateresco* style, where the door is framed by decorative stone. Most doors will have some metalwork detail, whether it be rusted studs, an enormous padlock, or a wrought iron knocker.

5

roofs

Mexican roofs not only provide protection against the elements, they reveal exquisite decorative detail too. Whether a mass of woven palm fronds, as in the thatched roofed *palapas* of the coast, or the more uniform terra-cotta tiles common in mountain towns, such as San Cristóbal de las Casas, the roof, more than any other architectural structure reveals creative but methodical workmanship. Roofs require the skill and knowledge of many generations: as in the working of palms for the *palapas* roof, the fronds are cut by the light of the moon, when they are at their most supple.

1

1 Waves of tiled roofs—a view of Morelia, from the Villa Montana Hotel. This city is so proud of its colonial architecture that any new building must accommodate and maintain the seventeenth-century look.

2 Traditional terra-cotta roof tiles from Sierra Nevada Hotel in San Miguel de Allende.

3, 5 & 7 Even eaves receive the bright color treatment, like these from San Cristóbal de las Casas.

4 Thin slivers of wood make up this highly patterned rooftop seen throughout southern Mexico. This is a reproduction of old housing in the Casa de las Artesanías in Morelia.

6 Palm frond thatching in the *palapas* style, near the Yucatán coastal town of Tulum. *Palapas* are the ultimate Mexican vernacular architecture, building from the natural environment in a style that hasn't changed for hundreds of years.

1 Painted tile and terra-cotta staircase in the house of potter Gorky González, in Guanajuato, designed by architect Manuel Parra.

2 Aztec royalty resided protected behind huge wooden doors at the top of an enormous staircase. Flowing from the second story like a symbolic illustration of Jacob's Ladder, this is perhaps the most famous staircase in recent Mexican architecture. They are cantilevered steps in Luis Barragán's own home in Mexico City.

3 In modern architecture, Barragán and others have paid homage to the ancient's use of the staircase, using materials such as black volcanic stone, contrasted against white walls. This is another set of stairs from Barragán's house. Carved from black volcanic stone, the stark contrast against the white walls is softened by the use of *rosa mexicana* along one wall.

4 Sweeping staircase rising from one floor to the next in a tiny hotel in San Miguel de Allende.

colonial

3 ▷

Taking just two years to conquer Mexico, the Spanish began building at a fast and furious pace. This need for speed was two-fold: the once glorious Aztec cities were now piles of rubble, and fast building work would aid continued domination, so that even at a glance, the Aztec population would be reminded of their newly conquered status. Much of the new architecture was designed by Franciscan monks who worked without plans, just from their memories of Spain, and built by the local population.

An average of one new church appeared every week in an effort to quickly convert the indigenous population to Catholicism. In essence, the style was large rooms supported by Roman columns, arches, and vaulted ceilings in classical proportions. Even the simplest of churches would contain at least one of these characteristics.

1 This is an original colonial arched doorway in the Sierra Nevada Hotel in Morelia. The hotel itself is made up of six restored colonial houses.

2 Vaulted ceilings and Roman columns are all classical touches which the Spanish revered. Symmetry in grand proportions was their architectural belief, and in Mexico it has remained so—even modern architects lean toward mathematical proportions and clean lines.

3 Guanajuato, in the state of Jalisco, is a city which prides itself on magnificent classical architecture. This was one of the richest cities in colonial times, making its money through the silver mines. The theater was built between 1873 and 1903, and while it may look classical on the outside, inside it is pure Moorish luxury.

1 An ornate facade in San Cristóbal de las Casas, showing classic colonial traits—turned columns, arched windows, and doorways with miniature statues inside a niche.

2 Casa de los Azulejos (the House of Tiles) in Mexico City. The outside wall is completely covered in tiles, the pattern only broken by a typical example of original *plateresco* from the late sixteenth century.

facades

The Spanish were architectural minimalists. The use of excessive decoration met with disapproval. Arches, columns, and classical dimensions without ornamentation, represented the building of the day. Except, that is, for the facade. In a style known as *plateresco*, the very front of the building, usually the frame around the door, was heavily embellished, in the same way as *plateros*, or the art of silver-smithing. The rest of the building frontage might be decorated using brightly colored tiles, half-turned columns, and niches for statuettes carved in brick.

2

3 The Maya also used facades at the front of important public buildings—painted with geometric symbols in bright reds and blues. This tradition of painting outside walls is evident today. Sunny yellow contrasted with lime green makes a cheerful facade of the front of this house in San Ángel.

4 Facades in Querétaro, an ancient town that made Mexican history when it became the center of a conspiracy to overthrow the Spanish-dominated government in 1810.

columns
and arches

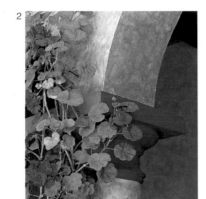

Columns and arches are a typical characteristic of the colonial style. Rows of columns usually provided support for a patio, which surrounded the courtyard and inner garden—a Moorish influence.

Arches were the established shape for the windows and doors of homes, while even the simplest church had an arched door, and high ceilings reaching toward the heavens.

1 Bridging the gap between indoors and out, this colonial patio with its classical columns and arches is in typical Spanish style. This is Casa Na Bolom, a well-known museum in San Cristobál de las Casas. It was originally the home of European explorers and anthopologists Frans Blom and Gertrude Duby.

2 Geraniums frame a colonial style column in a small restaurant in Oaxaca.

3 In true hacienda style, where architecture is on a grand scale, columns with an enormous girth line the patio at La Laja. The majority of the haciendas were damaged or burned down during the revolution. La Laja, however, remained fairly intact—its columns are originals from the sixteenth century.

2

hacienda

If there is one architectural statement that symbolizes the colonization of Mexico, it is the hacienda—a vast plot of land, encompassing acres of countryside with a house to match. There were many of these grand rural palaces built throughout Mexico between the sixteenth and eighteenth centuries, each operating as a mini state, run by a wealthy *hacendado* (owner) and his family. Most of them specialized in some kind of agriculture, using the surrounding population to maintain productivity

Each hacienda had a multitude of buildings to support the main house and the workers. These included stables, forges, a chapel, a school, and, of course, servants' quarters.

1 Hacienda La Laja outside Querétaro. This is one of the few original haciendas left standing. Many were burned or torn down after the Mexican Revolution. It has the characteristic cobbled stone courtyard surrounded by impressive stone walls, and round *ojo de buey* (ox eye) windows.

2 The kitchen of La Laja has "down-on-the-ranch" features such as cart wheels and ox heads mounted on the wall.

3 & 4 The chapel of La Laja. Acting as the social and political focal point for the surrounding areas, nearly all haciendas had a chapel.

beams

From ancient palaces to grand haciendas, wooden beams have lined ceilings, providing depth and structure to large-scale rooms. They were one of the first objects to be demanded by the Aztecs on neighborhood raids. As one of the primary conditions of surrender, a regular supply of large timber beams had to be delivered to their capital. As a tribute to both pre-Hispanic and colonial design, modern architects also favor the use of beams, but often on a more decorative level.

1 Former concrete sewage pipes pay architectural homage to wooden beams and mirror the rhythm of the staircase.

2 Traditional wooden beams make a comfortable contrast to the white walls in a house in Valle de Brava.

3 In a new take on an old theme, heavy wooden beams are replaced by a lighter look that creates a dance of light and shadow. The very modern look is found in José de Yturbe's house in Mexico City.

1, 2

3 ▷

palapas

Palapas, with their roofs of thatched palm fronds and rounded walls made of wooden slats, are created completely from natural elements.

The *palapas* is a common style of housing in jungle societies, but on the coast, they have also become a very popular form of modern-day housing, with architects and builders eliminating solid walls and doors altogether for a better enjoyment of air and views.

The basic shape and style of the *palapas* has remained unchanged with the passing of time. They have existed since ancient times, and will probably remain this way for centuries to come.

1 Hot from the pan: a feast of tortillas inside the cool *palapas*—no better way to escape the searing heat, while enjoying jungle views.

2 *Palapas* in the jungle, in Malpasito, in the state of Tabasco. This tiny community, high on the mountain known as El Mono Pelón (the Bald Monkey), live in resident palapas. A mountain spring provides running water, and bathing is in the river nearby.

1 The stone stairwell of la Casa de las Sirenas in Mexico City, which today is a restaurant, has an element of the Art Nouveau style in the stained glass window, seen on the right of the picture.

2 This fountain in a square in Querétaro has touches of the Baroque style, characterized by the statue and ornate decoration.

3 This ornate facade is typical of the French style with decorative twists of wrought iron for the balconies, opulent stone trimmings, and ornate window frames.

1

french style

Although the French were only in power for three years between 1864 and 1867, they left a legacy of style that is very apparent.

In 1865, following economic and social instability, Napoleon III appointed Maximillian as emperor. Politically, this proved disastrous, and Maximillian was executed three years later. Porfirio Díaz stepped in, ruling Mexico and encouraging European financial investment, and so Mexico continued to look toward France for guidance in style and architecture.

Huge French mansions were built in the neo-classical style, and art nouveau details such as wrought iron balconies with detailed swirls and beautiful stained glass windows became fashionable.

modern

With clean lines and bold colors, modern architects allow Mexico's natural materials to shine. Large expanses of volcanic stone across a courtyard; indigenous woods spanning a bright yellow wall; huge wooden beams dominating a ceiling, these are the kind of visual statements today's architects use to establish what has become known as a quintessentially modern Mexican look.

What characterizes the look is the cleanness and simplicity of the style of Luis Barragán, José de Yturbe, and Javier Sordo Madaleno, among others. Eschewing architectural detail, decoration often comes in the form of Mexican art, such as a grouping of large terra-cotta pots in a courtyard.

1 Strong use of color and angles at the modern Camino Réal Hotel in Mexico City, designed by architect Lagoretta.

2 Like the Maya, present-day architects such as José de Yturbe like to play with shadows and sunlight. Here the sun peeps through tiny holes in two very large rusted iron doors. Note the river stones on the floor, providing texture and unusual contrast with the more industrial looking door.

3 Pink shutters in Barragán's home, which is now the Casa Museo Luis Barragán. The bottom shutter can be left shut to block out the city while the top one is open to reveal the sky.

4 Smooth lines, dominated by bright colors. Here, the color of the desert, looks its best against a blue sky outside José de Yturbe's home in Mexico City.

5 Inviting the outside in—large horizontal windows provide optimum amounts of natural light. A yellow wall, with a floor of black volcanic stone, dramatically edged with white marble, defines the courtyard space in José de Yturbe's home in Mexico City.

5

furniture

The palaces and royal homes of the Aztecs were somewhat lavish with ornate furniture. Whole pieces of hardwoods carved into benches and tables, decorative wooden firescreens inlaid with gold figures and richly worked chairs covered with animal skins are just some of the types of furniture mentioned in Bernal Díaz's memoirs.

The Aztecs also showed a healthy disrespect for possessions. Believing in a life pattern of fifty-two years, they literally smashed their furniture to pieces on the eve of each new cycle . On the fifth and final day of the frenzy, the elders would look to the stars to guide them into a new age. Furniture and possessions were remade and preparations for a new life began.

When the Spanish conquered, they insisted the indigenous population learn the skills required to create their European styles of furniture. Elaborately carved armoires (wardrobe cabinets with doors) and turned leg tables became common. Colonial Mexico was also Spain's gateway to China, and thus absorbed some of the lavish styles of the Orient, particularly in regard to marquetry and other specialist inlaid techniques.

Classic designs have endured and are exported all over the world. Many of them, such as the *equipale* chair, are still handcrafted.

1 A chest of drawers from Yturbe's house in Mexico City. Smooth wooden planes are joined with simple dovetailing and contrasted with metal rings for handles.

chairs

In no other piece of furniture is there such variety of style than the simple chair. Mexican culture has long revered nature and lived in harmony with the natural world—only taking what is needed and leaving nothing to waste. Carvers work with the natural movement of wood: gnarled branches become the leg of a foot stool; entire trunks the seat of a chair. It has been this way for centuries. Designs may be hundreds of years old, but they still look good in a modern setting. The strong ladder-backed *cantina* chair, seen in restaurants across the country, is a practical choice grouped around the kitchen table, while the *equipale* chair, with its stretched pigskin back, and the *butaca* chair with its graceful curved form make more decorative furniture for the lounge or for relaxing on the patio, bridging the gap between indoors and out. On a more rudimentary level, the simple wooden stool is an extremely versatile item of seating.

1 Wooden stool from Hacienda Laleta, just outside San Miguel de Allende. Stools are the most common and practical of seats— they are designed as portable seating, and are carried everywhere, from the kitchen to the garden, or out to the market.

2 Fashioned from just two wooden pieces, this unusual three-legged chair has a carved hole at the top of the back rest for easy portability.

3 Mexico's most common chair— the ladder-back *cantina* chair. With its woven palm seat, it is used in restaurants throughout Mexico.

4 A patio area is furnished with *butacas* chairs. Its characteristic sling-back design dates from the sixteenth century. Traditionally the chairs are made from leather, although cane is sometimes used.

5 Solid colonial-design chairs from Hacienda La Laja. The *hacendados* were constantly entertaining, so there were several dining areas, each with plenty of furniture that had to be tough and durable. These chairs are made from hardwood, slung with leather that wears well with age.

6 Old style colonial chair from Casa Chata de Tlalpan in Mexico City. This straight-backed chair with solid arms was a style favored by the Spanish during the sixteenth and seventeenth centuries.

7 Simple and solid—the Mexican design rule for chairs. These sturdy chairs grace the dining room of potter Gorky González's home in Guanajuato.

8 The now world-famous *equipale* chairs. The barrel tops are usually handmade from pig skin, stitched and stretched over bench wood and attached to a base of slatted cedar. The chairs are held together with pine wood and glued where needed.

benches

Pausing to rest underneath an old mesquite tree, or just enjoying the sun in a private courtyard, *bancos* or benches, are one piece of furniture that no Mexican home is without. Even the most humble home will have an old bench without a back for the whole family to gather around the dinner table. Every *zócalo* and plaza has at least one bench inviting conversation between locals and serving as a meeting point for out-of-towners.

Made from woods such as cypress or mesquite, benches are often decorated with the popular scallop design along the edges of the back board and front of the seat, or with strong and eleborate cut out designs.

1 Long benches were first used in monasteries and grand public buildings. These matching benches are built in the colonial style and sit in the Villa Montana in Morelia. Their height is perfect for the low slung table.

2 This three-seater bench, from the Sierra Nevada hotel in San Miguel de Allende, looks like an extended colonial-style chair. It has a seat woven from rushes and the slats of the back are decorated with flowers.

3 This bench with a scalloped back board and front panel sits in the San Ángel district of Mexico City, an area known for its colonial touches and quiet corners.

4 This tiled bench looks as if it belongs next to a fountain in a garden, but it actually sits opposite an identical one in a covered alleyway in Querétaro.

◁ 1

built-in

There is no better way to make use of space than by building furniture into the walls. In what has become a very common design theme, walls are molded into chairs and benches which are then covered with extravagant cushions for comfort. This design scheme is most prevalent in the *palapas* style along the west coast, where chairs, beds, and benches become part of the architecture.

Built-in shelving accommodates the Mexican habit of collecting meaningful objects while ensuring rooms don't feel cluttered, and that valuable space is not lost. From hallways to bathrooms, niches and *trasteros* appear everywhere, holding treasured objects in their hollows and forming the perfect place for a mini altar. They are not just an interior feature, however, often appearing along garden walls, holding a stone sculpture or on the facade of a church framing a religious icon.

1 A built-in couch is complemented by a stone coffee table and paved floor, in a room that opens onto the garden. A set of upholstered *equipale* chairs completes the scene.

beds

For hundreds of years, Mexican beds were literally palm fronds woven into mats. Called *petates*, they were rolled out onto floors and benches for sleeping. They were also often carried by the bridal procession into church as a symbol of marital union. *Petates* remain common, especially in the countryside, but are sometimes replaced by a bed of bamboo splints stretched onto a framework of posts. Along the coast, it is common to see *hamacas* strung between two trees or posts. They are made of tough cotton and more recently colored nylon. During colonial times, ebony, mahogany, rosewood, and Spanish cedar were turned and carved into headboards, ensuring the rise of the bed's position as an ornate decorative retreat.

1 Flowing canopies over the bed has been a luxurious touch for centuries. As Bernal Díaz describes his bed at the Aztec palace in Tenochtitlán: "and for every one of us beds of matting with canopies above, and no better bed is given...". This canopied bed is in the Sierra Nevada hotel in San Miguel de Allende.

2 The hot pink cover on this bed is the only color in an otherwise neutral colored space. The design of the bed perfectly complements the simplicity of the room, with its components made up of natural materials.

3 Pure white bedding is in stark contrast to the warmth of this wood and brick-lined bedroom. The giant spindle-carved headboard is in a style common to the woodwork around Chihuahua City and the state of Zacatecas.

3 ▷

tables

The table is the one piece of furniture central to all of Mexico life. At the heart of the kitchen sits the *mesa de cocina* (kitchen table), the focal point of family meals and discussions; the table is central to the work-place; and it is the sole piece of furniture fundamental to the church—the *mesa de altar* or altar table. The majority of homes, too, will have an altar table, which becomes the focus of everyday prayer. Simple in design, the table is usually covered with treasured objects and offerings to God.

The style of tables varies from state to state. Querétaro has become the center for refined wood carving, with conservatively turned table legs and minimal decoration. In the state of Michoacán, tables are embellished with a more rustic look, known as chip or gouge carving, where chunks of wood are roughly cut creating simple patterns. Throughout central and western Mexico, the *mesa ranchero* (ranch style) table, with its square legs and solid top, is popular.

1 The formal dining room of an eighteenth-century house in San Miguel de Allende. The house's design is reminiscent of the ornate French-style popular at the time. The high-glossed table comfortably seats eighteen for a dinner party.

2 The *equipale*-style couch and wooden floor provide the perfect setting for this rustic coffee table.

3 Old doors and ancient wood pieces are often recycled to make new tables and other furniture items.

4 Modern designs take on sculptural forms, such as this table with a rusted iron base.

5 Decorative carving with restraint from this ancient dining room table in Villa Montana hotel in Morelia. Using techniques from across the world, as well as a background of pre-Hispanic tradition, Mexican wood carvers had developed quite a reputation by the eighteenth century.

cabinets and cupboards

There is no more personalized piece of furniture than the family chest. Usually made of *sabino* (Spanish cedar) or mesquite, it may be lined with cards of saints and photographs, sometimes scrawled with family signatures and pictures.

Trunks store blankets and clothes, while *trasteros* (cabinets), standing upright in the kitchen hold ceramic dishes, food, and wine. Elsewhere in the home, other storage furniture includes *roperos* (tall wardrobes)—the word *ropero* is derived from *ropa* meaning clothing—and *armarios*, the largest of cabinets with built-in drawers.

1 Antique merges with modern in the dining room of Casa Beryl, a house designed by José de Yturbe in Mexico City.

2 Family chests may be fashioned using rather simple woodworking skills, but inside they are often covered with family memorabilia and religious pictures, making them a living testament of family life through the generations. This old chest from a family house in Mexico City also displays treasured collections of bottles and *talavera* pieces.

3 Tiny drawers and intricate carving make for a distinctive chest on legs in the San Ángel Inn, a restored hacienda that is now a restaurant.

4 Inlaid woodwork became popular during the colonial period. This was a skill and influence learned from the Chinese—Mexico was a stop-off point from Spain to the East. This carved cupboard with colonial figures down each side is from Casa Amelia, a house designed by architect Agustin Hernández.

5 Hand-painted flowers decorate a crackle-glazed chest standing for sale outside a shop in Guanajuato.

6 Built-in storage cupboard in the house of potter Gorky González in Guanajuato. The open-plan design of the house means that cupboards and chests are invaluable.

gardens

In the fourteenth century, the Aztecs arrived in the Valley of Anáhuc (now the site of Mexico City), a mountain-ringed basin dotted with lagoons. They were forced to create yearly magical gardens to honor neighboring rulers. These took the form of floating gardens, covered in flowering bushes and juniper trees. More than a hundred years later, Aztec priests finally witnessed the much prophesized signal to build their own city—in the middle of Lake Toxcoc. As such, the Aztecs began to build what amounted to more giant floating gardens as foundation blocks. They constructed Tenochtitlán using tall cane sticks wedged into the mud, and reeds woven in between. More layers of mud were placed on top, and willow trees planted so that their roots would inter-twine with the reeds creating strong foundations for houses and palaces. The damp soil was especially fert-ile, and with their extensive knowledge of plants, the city became renowned for its marigolds, poinsettias, and exquisite trees. Examples of these "floating gar-dens" can be enjoyed today in the suburb of Xochimilco.

With the advent of colonialism, the intricate town planning of Tenochtitlán was completely redrawn, but in continuing the passion for gardens, every new town was designed with a plaza and every new home built with a courtyard full of trees and flowers.

1 Simplicity in an overgrown wilderness in the garden of Hacienda La Laja. The wagon adds a touch of traditional colonial to the greenery.

courtyards

The courtyard fulfills the Mexican desire for peace and privacy. Lying at the center of the house, all rooms face out onto this honored square of land, and a warm climate facilitates enjoyment of it all year round.

After the conquest, the courtyard and surrounding covered patio became an established architectural feature—homes, palaces, even monasteries enjoyed this inner sanctuary. Its paved surface often led to a central fountain, with the sound of running water providing further solitude. The origins of the courtyard is thought to be Moorish, and there has been some suggestion that the courtyard was favored in colonial times because the Spanish felt the need to protect themselves from warring Indians. This proved to be paranoia on the part of the colonials: in all states, with a few exceptions, the Indian population acquiesced to their newly conquered status.

1 In small courtyards, an earthenware pot with flowering bougainvillea are all that are desired to create a sense of garden.

2 Steps lead down to the courtyard with walls enlivened with *rosa mexicana*. As a modern touch, a criss-cross of beams is seen overhead.

3 A dramatic accent in a corner of a courtyard in architect José de Yturbe's house. The strong shapes of blue agave plants complement the volcanic stone floor and contrast with the bright yellow and orange walls.

4 A typical colonial courtyard, dominated by a surrounding patio of high arches, columns, and balconies in Tlalpan, a suburb in Mexico City. The courtyard is of an original design—patterned stonework on the ground leading to a central fountain.

5 A high arch covered in foliage marks the entrance to this courtyard in the Sierra Nevada Hotel in San Miguel de Allende.

patios

In Mexican architecture, much is made of the relationship between opposites—public and private, light and shade, and in the case of the patio, indoors and out. Framing the courtyard, the patio is the architectural bridge between the garden and the house. With the overhead ceiling supported by large Romanesque columns and classical arches, stylistically the patio hasn't altered through the ages. It is a direct copy from the Moors, and similiar designs can be seen in Southern Spain, although the Mexican patio tends to be bigger than its Andalucian cousin. The floor is usually made from chunks of hand-cut stone or cobbles, and is often graced with terra-cotta pots and climbing vines.

1 With the warm climate, patios literally become outdoor rooms, with permanent furniture grouped for socializing. This impressive patio is at Hacienda Laleta, but even the most lowly of homes will have a wooden bench out on the patio.

2 Symmetrical wooden beams are ubiquitous on the ceilings of patios, such as these from a hotel in Oaxaca.

3 Sky blue and terra-cotta paintwork gives the patio of this colonial museum a fresh look. Casa Na Bolom in San Cristóbal de las Casas, was once the home of Danish explorers and anthropologists, and has become an intellectual center for the region.

4 Classical columns receive some eyecatching paintwork at another hotel In San Cristóbal de las Casas.

water features

Water has been worshipped throughout Mexico as a magical, mystical source of life for centuries. Oceans, mountain streams, and springs were the focus of religious ritual, for water was not only treasured for obvious agricultural blessings, but also for its ceremonial purity. Water, pure and holy, is used in Catholic baptisms, and also played a correlative role in Aztec and Mayan ceremonies where babies were purified.

In private places the fountain is the focus of the courtyard; in public spaces it can be found in most plazas and on many street corners. Although of Spanish descent, the Mexican fountain has a look all of its own. It is usually covered in *azulejos* (tin-glazed tiles), and shaped as a rectangle, hexagon, octagon or circle with the outer pool a repeat of this pattern.

The Baroque style of the seventeenth century saw fountains becoming the focus of a rich ornamentation, that was often eschewed in other architectural areas. The fountain was not just covered in tiles, but was decorated with carved statuettes spilling water and given multi-layered stone bases.

In modern architecture, water remains a symbol of serenity. Today's architects like to contrast the fountain with the use of large expanses of still water. This offers a space of calm reflection, often mirroring the use of bright colors.

1 At the Egerström ranch, water cascades in a large pond from a chute set into a high wall that mirrors the architectural style of the complex.

2 Throughout Mexican towns, a fountain is never far away. This one stands in Morelia.

3 The fountain, surrounded by stone paths edged with greenery means this symmetrical courtyard takes on a rather formal design in the Sierra Nevada Hotel.

4 Water provides serenity away from the city hubbub at this poolside view in the Villa Montana outside Morelia.

5 Modern architect Lagoretta creates movement in an otherwise still courtyard with a bubbling whirlpool at the Camino Réal hotel in Mexico City.

6 Strong angles and still water create a quiet corner at this house in Valle de Brava. The vibrancy of the yellow walls is beautifully contrasted by the blue tiles of the pool.

7 Calm contemplation—water seemingly without depth in a courtyard of dark paving stones edged with white marble.

garden scenes

"We must not forget the gardens of flowers and sweet-scented trees...and the walks and the ponds and tanks of fresh water." Bernal Díaz.

Whether it be a dirt courtyard with a couple of bougainvillea beds or myriad tree-lined paths and flowering waterways, Mexican gardens reflect an instinctive relationship with the natural world. Plants are not shaped and controlled, but guided along stone walls; branches of huge trees twist and turn free of human guidance. Walls and *citerallas* (open brick patterned walls), patterned paving, and tiled fountains all feature as punctuation marks within the greenery, and garden sculptures reside in overgrown vines.

1 Colorful birdcages and potted
flowers line the wrought iron balcony
of a home in San Miguel de Allende.
Balconies often boast excellent
views over the courtyard.

2 Natural stone, terra-cotta, and
wood create a rustic scene in Casa
Lisa's garden in San Miguel de
Allende.

3 In the same way a Mexican home
is a place to house unusual but
collectible objects, so too is the
garden. Old stone sculptures,
figures, and posts appear amidst
the foliage. This large clay pot, in the
garden of Casa Lisa, is actually an
old oven.

4 Leafy palms and stone walkways create an exotic garden at Casa Na Bolom in San Cristóbal de las Casas. The corner light makes an ingenious, if a little unusual, use of a terra-cotta pot.

5 The garden holds a sacred and symbolic place at the heart of Mexican culture. Even before Catholicism's Eden, the garden was the focus of ancient creation myths. The Mixtecs, Oaxaca's indigenous people, believed they were born into the most exquisite and fragrant garden of scattered petals and flowering bushes.

6 & 7 The Mexican love of color extends to its beautiful blooms. Hundreds of years ago the Aztecs lavished much energy on their gardens full of magnificent flowers, which remain popular today.

8 Garden courtyards often convey an ordered simplicity, with plants and trees growing from containers. In this garden in San Miguel de Allende, pots neatly line the terra-cotta wall.

9 The branches of this plant have been encouraged to intertwine to create an attractive latticework that actually gives the climbing plant extra strength to stand upright.

10 Broken crockery pieces are recycled on garden furniture at the home of architect José Luis Cortes.

11 Tall cacti make the perfect natural fence guarding privacy in the suburb of San Ángel in Mexico City.

credits

The publishers would particularly like to thank Martin Ruiz Camino and Lupita Ayala at the Mexican Ministry of Tourism in London and Martin's wife Tony for their generous help and support in arranging the itinerary for Peter Aprahamian in Mexico.

In Mexico, we would like to thank SECTUR for organizing access to museums including the Museo Nacional de Antropolgia and other institutions, José Luis Cortes, José de Yturbe and Enrique Martin Moreno, Augustin Hernandez, Rodolfo Ogarrio, Jorge Favela, and Miquel Adria for setting up introductions, and to all those people who opened their doors and helped Peter with the photography.

Grateful thanks go to the Casa-Museo Luis Barragán, to Norma Soto and to the Egerström and Prieto López families for the access to the Barragán works. The photographs of these properties on pages 12, 35, 39, 62, 73, 83, 90, 108, and 134 were reproduced by permission of The Barragán Foundation, the Instituto Nacional de Bellas Artes and the owners of the houses.

Luis Barragán's Home and Studio, designed by architect Luis Barragán in 1947 in Tacubaya, Mexico City, is a property of Gobierno de Jalisco and Fundación de Arquitectura Tapatía Luis Barragán, tel and fax: (52) 5 515 4908, e-mail: cmlbmex@df1.telmex.net.mx.

The Barragán Foundation takes care of Luis Barragán Archives and copyrights, Barragán Foundation, 20 Klünenfeldstrasse, CH-4127, Birsfelden, Switzerland, e-mail: barragan.foundation@vitra.com.

The hotels Villa Montana in Morelia, Sierra Nevada in San Miguel de Allende, and Camino Réal in Mexico City on pages 21, 30, 39, 42, 60, 88, 89, 92, 108, 116, 117, 121, 123, 131, 135, 136, and 137 were photographed by kind permission of Exsus Travel Limited. We would like to thank Melanie Cutcliffe at Indigo Public Relations Limited for making the arrangements.

Exsus Travel Limited, a new upmarket tour operator specializing in tailor-made holidays to Mexico, South America and the Caribbean, offers clients quality, exclusivity and a truly personalized service when planning their itinerary. For a copy of their glossy brochure, contact Exsus on Tel: 020 7292 5050/Fax: 020 7292 5051 or email: travel@exsus.com.

bibliography

Allan, Tony, Tom Lowenstein, Dr Tim Laughton, *Gods of Sun and Sacrifice—Aztec and Maya Myth*, Duncan Baird Publishers, 1997.

Castaneda, Carlos, *Journey to Ixtlan the Lessons of Don Juan*, Arkana Penguin Books, 1990.

Díaz del Castillo, Bernal, *The Discovery and the Conquest of Mexico: 1517–1521*, translated from the Spanish by A. P. Maudslay, Da Capo Press, New York, 1996.

Kirby, Rosina Greene, *Méxican Landscape Architecture From the Street and From Within*, University of Arizona, Tucson, 1972.

Levick, Melba, Tony Cohan and Masako Takahashi, *Mexicolor*, Chronicle Books, 1998.

Mexico Lonely Planet Survival Kit, Lonely Planet Publications, Jul 1995.

Mexico The Rough Guide, The Rough Guides, Jan 1999.

Miller, Mary and Karl Taube, *An Illustrated Dictionary of the Gods and Symbols of Ancient Mexico and the Maya*, Thames and Hudson, 1997.

Paz, Octavio, *The Labyrinth of Solitude*, translated from the Spanish by Lysander Kemp, Yara Milso and Rachel Phillips Belash, Penguin Books, 1990.

Rosoff Beimler, Rosalind, *The Days of the Dead*, Pomengranate Europe Ltd, 1991/1998.

Sanford, Trent Elwood, *The Story of Architecture in Mexico . . .*, W. W. Norton &, New York, 1947.

Sayer Chloë, *Arts and Crafts of Mexico*, Thames and Hudson, London, c. 1990.

Shipway, Verna Cook, *The Mexican House, Old & New*, Architectural Book Publishing Company, New York, 1960.

Street-Porter, Tim, *Casa Mexicana*, Stewart, Tabori & Chang, 1989.

Witynski, Karen and Joe P. Carr, *Mexican Country*, Gibbs Smith, Publisher, 1997.

Ypma, Herbert, *Mexican Contemporary*, Thames and Hudson, 1997.

index